City in a Seashell

New Women's Voices Series, No. 180

poems by

Tiffany Osedra Miller

Finishing Line Press
Georgetown, Kentucky

City in a Seashell

New Women's Voices Series, No. 180

ACKNOWLEDGMENTS

I am so grateful for the ongoing inspiration of my wonderful parents. This
book would not exist without the legacy of their humor, mystery, beauty and
genius. Even though I never knew I could miss anyone as much as I miss
them, I find immense joy, hope and solace in writing about them. I dedicate
City in a Seashell to their memory.

Many thanks to Peggy Gould, Denise James, Laura James, Pamela Joyce,
Leyla Modirzadeh, Michael Rogers, Liz Werner and Gary Wood for many
years of feedback, encouragement and support.

Many thanks to Josh Roark, Wendy Lesser, the Hurston Wright Foundation,
Mat Johnson, Ed Bullins, Jacqui Henderson and all of my current and former
students who really are some of my greatest teachers.

A huge appreciation for my dear Aunt Paula, Sara and Paul Kliger for
sharing their encouragement and enthusiasm for my writing.

And of course, thank you to the wonderful, supportive staff at Finishing Line
Press!

Publisher: Leah Huete de Maines
Editor: Christen Kincaid
Cover Art: "Maroonlight Cantata"(2013) by Tiffany Osedra Miller
Author Photo: Gary D. Wood
Cover Design: Elizabeth Maines McCleavy

Order online: www.finishinglinepress.com
also available on amazon.com

Author inquiries and mail orders:
Finishing Line Press
PO Box 1626
Georgetown, Kentucky 40324
USA

Contents

In Memory of my Dear, Sweet, Mother and Father

The Dream of Being Together

We have officially forgotten Sunday, when after
church, we cheeky, American-born children once
devoured seasoned saltfish with savory johnnycakes
and drank the red sorrel and goat water our
Caribbean Grandmothers left for us on islands of
elbow-greased windowsills uptown in New York City

We have forgotten how frozen palm trees
garnished our row house rum punch. Sunday
night metropolis-moonshine. Family jammin'
barefoot to Christian and Un-Christian Calypso
on the polished, living room dancehall floor

Who knew that one day most of us could only
dream of being together again, breaking breadfruit
inside sacred and profane row house sandcastles
loosely built beneath the Big Sugar Apple Stars

City in a Seashell

You would be surprised to find inside of a seashell the
presence of peacock covered pineapple trees, sultry cities
preserved like primitive line drawings carved into
sweet, sugar apple walls. Each raindrop, a reveler,
each teardrop, tinsel from the timeless, tropical tree

The City, of course, has a Sunday School on each
corner full of the blackberry liqueur of violet psalms

the City in the Seashell with its purple trellises full
of calypso-caroling boys dragging their fat blueberries up
the trellis to the veranda or fire escape to serenade a swarthy
siren at an open window

this is not quite a story about where she's from or how she
got there. It is more an account of a walk, a promenade
through an island girl's merry and melancholy metropolis

The Drummer in the Immaculate Room

Once, during the annual pre-Lenten Caribbean Carnival, she encountered a man as dark and dashing as her grandfather, drumming in the center of a large, immaculate room. But she couldn't hear a single drumbeat because her ears were not adjusted to the frequency of that sound. And she could usually hear everything—a red feather, floating through the island's quietest night. Crooked crickets, sworn to silence, after they witnessed a murder of crows. Pineapple milk flowing from a pineapple tree into the calypso of the Jo-coconut River. Solemn, stilt walker spirits strolling, then hovering in meditation, just above the wretched, incredible earth.

She wondered if the drummer was her actual grandfather, who died long before she was born, and whose picture she never saw. All she knew—from what her mother told her—was that he was as dark as the magnificent, melanated night and that he was a fisherman who died at sea when her mother was a little girl.

And what if the drummer wasn't making any sound at all, even though seeing a man hit a drum would suggest that he was creating the vibration of music. When he smiled at her from where she gazed at his kind, immaculate face through the Caribbean carnival window, she was almost sure he was her mother's father.

But if she could hear her grandfather's drumbeats—if the drummer indeed was he—and if she could tune in to the proper frequency of those ancestral echoes, rhythmic, rhapsodic fables, powerful, primitive parables of sound—what would they tell her of his hard life and his life after life and her life and would she listen.

Outrageous Stories and Sunken Ships

My father's father was born on an island floating on a sea of outrageous stories and sunken ships. When I encountered him at carnival, fully costumed and masked to look the way he did in his life, he recognized me as his granddaughter, bowed before me and called himself a storyteller. He then proceeded to tell me about characters who suddenly appear in the stories that we tell.

Characters are ancestors wearing different disguises
and are often of a different design.
During carnival, we call them revelers.

To get to carnival that year, he said he had crawled out of a broken grandfather clock located at the Plantation Museum. He then sat at the edge of a fountain facing away from the world he left behind. He rolled up his trousers so he could dangle his cornmeal colored limbs in the fountain-water. At the center of the fountain—a statue of his son—eternal acolyte, infinite soldier, my father. Nearby, my grandfather's carousel horse waited in meditation beneath a holiday tree.

Delighted, I danced with my grandfather. A full island girl. Not one trace of city. Pineapple milk flowed joyously from my breasts into the calypso of the Jo-coconut River. With one hand, I drew across the starry sky, an even better blueprint for my life. With the other hand, I held—on top of my head—a Caribbean carnival urn full of ancestral ashes, outrageous stories, sunken ships.

Climb the Sugar Apple Staircase

Longing to *Fête* and *Form the Fool?* Yearning to leave your cold city for the balmy, bacchanalian heat of the Gabindan Isles, but world events and personal circumstances render you unable to? Well you can visit Gabinda for free if, while trudging through the streets of your cold city, you locate the Sugar Apple Staircase and descend its winding, wintry steps into royal blue darkness until your cold, weary feet finally touch the burning equator.

Feel the merciful heat, hold tight to the bannister, round a corner and board a Sugar Apple Streetcar to a different section of the staircase. Climb three more labyrinthine levels until you reach Gabinda, the island home of garish, Goatwateresque carnivals, angels, ancestors and acolytes located in the Sugarcane Region of the Caribbean. Gabinda, obscured behind veils, jo-coconut waterfalls and mists, remains invisible to the untrained eye, the untutored soul, as explorers and conquerors never located it during their peregrinations. They had, however read and heard stories about Gabinda's peculiar beauty and enigmatic occupants frequently enjoying their masked, calypsonian bacchanals from run down tenement yards to sun-kissed and moon-embraced ballrooms perched along cliffs overlooking the beach.

Once you arrive in Gabinda, acolytes will greet you wearing God's motley on their wooly heads. Long, colorful Guayabera shirts cover their torsos. They swing the sweetest incense and carry large illuminated crosses and Caribbean candles to light your way. Stunning stilt walkers wearing animal-masks, dance like giraffes through the Gabindan bush, where brown, barefaced butterfly women rest their wondrous wings. For awhile, let glorious Gabindan peacocks push aside the pensive pigeons of your cold intense city. Dine with revelers dressed as Dame Lorraine and Jab Molassie those red devils, who after dancing sensually all night— eat with their post-colonial pitchforks English and Gabindan breakfasts of blood pudding, beans, saltfish and chips.

The Gorgeous Ghost of my Father

I have often heard certain story-songs emanate from the
bayous of Louisiana and whenever I slept with my lover
amongst the sacred and sensual sins of the moonlit swamps.
I heard these songs while roller-skating down the hill,
past the playground before crossing beneath the bridge at
Bronx Park, where years later, I encountered the gorgeous
ghost of my father jogging up and down the Sugar Apple
Staircase. Every illuminated step he took, I saw—carved into
the ancient staircase—his ink and pastel drawings of the
dazzling impossibilities of possible dreams.

The Dusky Cherubs

Ethereal, island mothers, after partially immaculate conceptions, pull their offspring—dusky, sweet-faced cherubs—out of the burning, Gabindan mud. The newborn cherubs, perspiring in the heat, yearn for the cold weather of northern cities where warm-blooded-immigrants dress in heavy coats. *How cold could it be?* the cherubs mused. Overheated, and therefore eager to know, they fly up the Sugar Apple Staircase to attend a Caribbean ice carnival. As soon as they arrive, the cold air silences their cherub-songs. Shivering, the cherubs wander the city searching for merciful souls to pour cocoa tea for them with a tit of rum. Despite their baby faces, Gabindan cherubs are not children. They are the dusky, adventuresome angels of Gabinda.

The cherubs nibble on peanut cakes, drink cocoa tea and listen to old calypso inside cozy cafés. Outside, they ride carousel horses covered in snow. The cherubs coax warm caresses and cuddles from cold-hearted strangers, then fall asleep curled up on cold, star-lit windowsills. When these cheeky, dimpled, Gabindan angels discover their wings have frozen, they endeavor to return to Gabinda. The cherubs quickly find the Sugar Apple Staircase, which leads them to their warm, balmy island abodes. Ecstatic, the cherubs embrace their native sun, then fly to bacchanals taking place beneath Gabinda's warmest, blue-green seas.

Back in the Gabindan bush, the cherubs are joined by acolytes and choirs of children dressed as psalm-birds. Headdresses full of feathers and scripture adorn their plaited heads. The choir offers baskets of sugar apples and mangoes. They open treasure chests full of wooden storytellers and cloth effigies of Midnight Robbers, ready to tell their tall tales. With their Gabindan faces rosy as dark, red chocolates, the children—and cherubs—open their maroon mouths to sing: *Bacchanalia! Hallelujah!*

Church of the Tree Frogs

An acolyte, in need of silence, prayer and scripture, carries candles across an open field. No sign of cars, Christians, or collection plates only tree frogs, ancestral chariots and captive choirs singing silently in carriages that appear and fade away. God's garden grows behind a translucent wall. A one-time waterfall, sudden and silent, passes on. The church has closed its doors and applied the latch. The hymns, hushed. Even the sunflowers blush scarlet, then violet.

The acolyte encounters several tree frogs, lit up like fireflies amidst a group of leafy trees, huddled close, gathering their thoughts. The acolyte unsure of what to do, taps on the bark of the first tree. The tree trunk, with a welcoming spirit, opens up like a door. Anointed elephants, giraffes, and a host of sparrows, march out.

A staircase unfurls within the tree. A light, from a much brighter and deeper candle shines within. Tree frogs, wearing solid green crosses, silently greet and accompany the acolyte down the bright staircase into the healing light.

Johnnycakes #1

*

A Johnnycake is a short, savory, sweet,
sensual, and at times, spiritual, pensive
or sanguine poem, fragment or story
with Caribbean-American themes.
A Johnnycake is also a savory dumpling
as well as a voluptuous woman of St. John's
harboring big macatampas in her sundress

*

St. John's is the capital of Antigua, W.I.
where my dear, sweet, mother—a cheeky
nurse known throughout her Bronx hospital as
Jean the Queen, Miller the Killer—was born

*

Antiguan acolytes, marching in morning
light bearing crosses
Jamaican soldiers, marching at midnight,
bearing arms

*

A fine, wooden, infant figurine emerges from a
whittler's hands to come of age on an altar

*

Sailing with Saint John on Saint John's Eve
along a radiant river of Revelations

*

A stilt walker lost in a northern city
peers into a skyscraper window

*

My mother—her hair in long, loose pigtails—
her belly big and pregnant with me,
shuffles joyously up the steep,
wooden staircase in St. John's, Antigua.

*

Without my late father's, Jamaica or
my dear, departed, mother's, Antigua
there would be no enchanted
islands of Gabinda or Conjoo
re-discovered waiting within
the Goatwaterfalls and waves of my grief

*

St. John told me that when my mother ran up
the Sugar Apple Staircase for the last time that
she left the *Book of Revelation* for me on the seventh step.
When I retrieved the sacred book, I was shocked to find
that it was titled the *Book of Revelers*, instead.
And it began with a tale about a valiant, holy horse—
a half breed carousel marvel made of golden, cornmeal-colored
wood and white flesh—and his horseman, my paternal
grandfather

*

To attend a Dream Carnival, you must
cross mythological railroad tracks
laid in labyrinths across the equator
until you reach the Carnivalesque
Caribbean of the deep, mystical south

How to Plan a Tea Party

I said this to Carlo:
How wonderful it would be to take our mothers to tea.
After all, your mother was born in the Bronx.
My mother died in the Bronx.

Your mother in her new life, would be summoned
by the call of the Sacred Cardinal, with a flourish.
My mother, would come to us from her new life,
where she lives in a palace surrounded by ceramic ducks.

But how nice it would be to take them to the Village for tea.
We would feed them mince meat pies, scones, curried salmon,
We would petition the kitchen, to carry in for them any
kind of caviar. Scones with jam, cream, custard, caramel.

Fruity teas with fresh cream and sugar. Irish Breakfast tea
with just a splash of whisky. Creamy, Caribbean Cocoa tea with a
tit of rum. Blood pudding. Codfish cakes. Fish and chips.
Platters of persimmon, mango, pineapple,
watermelon and sweet pear.

We would dab their rouged lips
with their own heaven-sent handkerchiefs
covered in obscure mathematical patterns,
rooted in the Beatitudes, Psalms and other scripture.

Our mothers would speak to us of infinite
gardens of Grace that are more than gold
and green and not at all less than sublime.

And, we would all laugh, together, Carlo,
at life's absurdities, human foibles,
misunderstandings, fumbles.

You and I would laugh about this until our sides hurt. And our beloved mothers, would laugh, mercifully, drinking their assorted teas together, devouring the savory, succulent, sweet gifts from their children without feeling any pain.

The Calypsonian Sea Woman

During Carnival in the Caribbean,
on a starlit evening,
steeped in darkness, desire and delight,
a woman emerged from the sea
playing calypso on a Spanish guitar
as she approached the island shore

An elder was sleeping on the beach before her
beside him, a large bottle, tipped over.
Red wine stained the golden sand. She sang:

Aye, Aye, Aye, Aye, Oh my...Oh my...

A horse, neighed in the darkness
and trotted over to the sleeping elder.
The horse, dressed for carnival,
looked curiously at the sea woman
who lingered at the shore line
playing calypso on her Spanish guitar. She sang:

Aye, Aye, Aye, Aye,
How many ships have passed us by?
How many lips have said goodbye?
How many birds no longer fly?

The horse, with tears in his eyes, danced,
shaking the colorful bells tied about his head
and around his hoofs. She continued:

Hear what I say,
you must pray before you play
then you can jam and dingolay

The man, roused by the unusual celebration,
sat up and rubbed the sleep from his eyes.
He encountered the woman, singing
and his horse, dancing

"What is going on here, Quincy?
the man asked his horse.
"Drink made my head so fooly,
bam-boozle-dy and bazodee.
Who the devil is this lady?"

He put the bottle to his mouth
searching for more wine.
"Quincy, answer me!" he hollered,
and the horse whimpered and neighed.
"Madame, who are you?" the man asked her
and threw the empty bottle into the sea.
"You seem familiar."

The sea woman replied:
"I am the child of your child.

My dear father was your son.
He buried you long before I was born.
I've drowned in this sea twice,
therefore, the Underwater is my home.
Hello Grandfather."

The man glanced at his pocket watch.
"Too much drink. Too much drink!" he said,
and climbed on top of Quincy's back
and rode away as fast as he could.

The next night, Quincy,
this time wearing motley,
trotted back to the sea, alone.

Aye, Aye, Aye, Aye,
How many lips have said goodbye...

Sang the sea woman, at the shore
playing calypso on her Spanish guitar.

Caribbean-American Dream Renaissance

Most Sundays of my youth, church officials handed out to all of the congregants—who were mostly Jamaican or of Jamaican descent—small, square cards, the size of Cricket trading cards featuring full color reproductions of religious, Renaissance paintings. The alternate side of each card featured the Biblical story behind the painting. These paintings were originally created on huge canvases with oils by Master European artists of the 16th century, such as Raphael, DaVinci and Michelangelo. The church officials inserted these cards within church leaflets, which announced recent death notices, donations, birthdays, shut-ins, trips to museums, dinner theater, seafood at City Island, gambling at Atlantic City.

These Renaissance cards, though seemingly thin and flat, held such depth and dimension for me—*The Last Supper, The Annunciation.* More than tiny card stock print outs of large-scale paintings they contained universes of possibility much like the universes my mother carried throughout her native island of Antigua inside of a bucket perched upon her head. Other islanders believed she carried wares from the market, coconuts, or holy water. Inside these baskets were staircases leading to impossible landscapes, unfathomable seascapes and Caribbean-American Dream Carnivals.

This same church, years later, officiated my mother's funeral. What remained of her was hidden inside a closed casket in front of the altar, while her luminous soul ascended the casket's staircase into Heaven, where she was ordained Carnival Queen at the most Sacred and Supreme Carnival.

Johnnycakes #2

*

Dancing close together
in a lush paradise of Gabindan bush:
one red, sweet, almighty mango
and a tall, thick, tender, stalk of sugarcane

*

Jesus, I saw a goat beheaded
on the side of an Antiguan Road.
How come I will never be the same?

*

Where are you, Grandma Wilhelmina?
Are you in the garden full of
glass houses, cathedrals and goats?
Are you with my mother?

*

I heard that another earth exists inside
the candle flame flickering above
a cylinder of thick wax on top of my
Grandmother's ancient
Book of Common Prayer

*

Weeping in St. John's, Antigua, I walk
Fort Road to Fort Beach
with the ghosts of my mother and father

*

"The pleasures of Paradise,"
the painted Priestess
of the Calypsonian Crosswalk began,
"are found not only in the heavens,
these pleasures also exist on
the Secret Streets of St. John's, Antigua
inside of markets carrying coveted
sugar apples, which contain the
sweetest, juiciest, pulpiest walls"

*

I've read some of the most
primitive poetry and lyrics
recorded in pidgin and patois
inside *The Jungle Song Book*

Sea of White Goats

After weeks of paradise and Carnival parades in Antigua, where I was regularly chased by teenaged saga boys, lusty lizards and horny goats, I—not quite a teenager myself—reluctantly returned home to the Bronx and wandered over to the shopping plaza, a formidable area haunted by drug addicts and pushers.

That evening, a trumpeter introduced a church revival in the plaza's parking lot. The Holy Rollers attempted to root out the devil with song and testimony while families shopped for groceries. The Rollers, Caribbean immigrants to the U.S., wore white, which contrasted with their dark skin—*dark as Antigua at dusk*—so says the Calypso. I recalled a sea of white goats rushing towards me in St. John's, Antigua as I skulked among its shadows and secret streets.

Terrified, I ran like an Olympian and hurtled over a fence onto a porch. Thankfully, the goats ignored me as they were headed someplace else. I felt foolish, of course, as those who witnessed the scene cackled with laughter. I, too, laughed at myself. Hardly back in the Bronx a full day, I already longed for the wild beauty, absurd humor and mystical carnival of my Mother's native island of Antigua.

A Caribbean immigrant Auntie dressed in white approached me in the parking lot. In one hand, she held a Bible. In the other hand, she held a Bible. On her head she carried a stack of Bibles. *What's a nice, young girl like you doing here, in the Devil and dem's, Parking Lot?* she asked me. Her accent thick, I could sense her longing to return to Antigua. I shrugged and ran away from her to search for deep, tropical basements full of brown, bacchanalian saga boys, virgin rum, oceans, mango and aloe.

In Bronx basements, full of the mythological memories of Caribbean islands, missed and longed for, immigrant aunties, playing the masque of being back home, sell rum, sorrel, tamarind balls and peanut candy along the side of the dusty basement road.

Behind the washing machine—a ghost cousin washes clothes the old, Antiguan way—with a rustic, washboard and basin—then hangs the clothes on a clothesline, just like she is back home on her beloved island again. Beneath the battered, basement light, turned on by a gentle tug of a palm leaf, Rasta men capture runaway goats and behead the great white beasts to make goat water in the kitchenette. The same Rasta men dig mass graves beneath the mildewed basement tiles for New York's carnival kings and queens who had expired in New York City winters, whereas they flourished in Antigua's endless summers.

In the Villa Area of Antigua,
white goats, fall into the sea
after chasing through the dusty roads
and streets a girl called, Epiphany.

Revive the Caribbean revelry—
every night in New York City
make us dizzy with drink,
dance and bazodee!—so says the
girl called Epiphany...

We don't want to be Metropolitan,
because the sky above the sea is sparkling,
crickets are calling, sea goats are swimming.
Soca spirits of celebration are marching up
the basement steps onto the city streets!

The Riderless Horse: (film notes for my father)

("The Riderless Horse" was originally a
mural that my father wanted me to paint
on his living room wall. What started out
as his reverie became my recurring dream.
My father—a small child peering out of a
window from a house in Jamaica watching
his distressed, inebriated father leave on
horseback—only to witness many hours later,
the horse return to the house without its rider.

How could I have painted my father's first
heartbreak? While I never painted the mural
before he passed away, I have written down
its essence in poetic, dream carnival form,
even envisioning this formative memory as a
film which begins in New York and takes
us back to my father's Jamaica)

-New York City: Henry Maxwell stumbles out of a taxi. Two
wooden figurines loiter in shadows across the street on top of an
altar in front of a laundromat. Henry climbs the staircase to his
building. He unlocks the outer door and retrieves his mail from
the mailbox. He unlocks the inner door and enters the dark lobby,
which is as quiet as St. John's Cathedral.

-*Henry?* A woman with an island accent, calls out. She emerges
from the staircase, holding a platter of tea lights. She wears a white
dress so textured it reminds Henry of a corrugated roof. African
violets adorn the sleeves of her dress. She places the platter of tea
lights between them on the floor and steadies a basket of sugar
apples on top of her head. Her features, lovely, yet unclear in the
dark. Her head, the silhouette of a palm leaf. *How does she know
my name?* Outside, a sudden downpour.

-*Henry Maxwell?*
-*Henry? I don't know who that is.*
-*Where then, is the man with your name?*

She asks, pointing at a large envelope in his hands, addressed to:
Henry Maxwell.

-I was told he lived in this building.
-I don't know him.
-Please give this card to Mr. Maxwell

A white business card pierces the darkness.
Blank except for a phone number scribbled
in ink and a scripture: John 3:16

-What would I tell him this is all about? It's well
after midnight—

-A woman would like to question Henry
about the disappearance of his father.
Her grandfather.   .

-And who are you? Are you that woman?
-Yes. I am Henry's daughter, she says, picks
up her tea lights and swiftly exits the building.

Breathless. A cold sweat. Henry takes off his trench coat and suit
jacket. *Henry's daughter! My daughter?* He opens the front doors
and runs outside in the rain. He opens the envelope to find a
photograph of his daughter in silhouette. *Miss! Miss! Daughter!*
Daughter! he cries out. But she had already gone away.

Flashback: Henry's distraught father in Jamaica
leaving their house on horseback, to search for drink.
Little Henry waits all night by the window. Near dawn,
the horse returns home without Henry's father—

Close up:
The altar with two figurines in front of
the laundromat. Father and son. Seashells, a small
ceramic ship, a glass horse, a wooden grandfather
clock, an offering of dark rum in a shot glass.

The sound of a horse galloping and neighing.
Frightened, Henry returns to his building.
At the lobby window, he pulls back the curtain.

The horse, without a rider, appears on the road.
Henry's daughter, illuminated by tea lights, mounts
the magnificent, horse. The horse rears up on its
hind legs, lands on all fours and gallops away.

Biography of my Babysitter's Daughter

My babysitter often
beat her beautiful
dark brown, teenaged daughter
with an old mean broom
while my brother and I
drew street lamps
in our sketchbooks
to light their gloomy living room

My babysitter's daughter—
eventually ran away
packed her church hat and
her liquor bottle
before the grim light of another day

She rode the train from
the Bronx to Coney Island.
Witnessed baby-faced gangsters—
break soda bottles over sleeping heads.

Later, my babysitter's daughter
managed to get a job
changing the soiled linens on top of
filthy rich people's, king-sized beds

She slept on starless side streets
then found a way to sleep inside—
multiple, merciful chapels and churches
on the lower east side

She rented a room without electricity.
After work, beneath freezing, flickering
street lamps—hunger in her tired eyes—
she'd read technicolor books about Utopias,
Dreamlands and Paradise

She'd press her nose against café windows
craving a coffee, a piece of toast,
a companion, or just an avocado pear
but whenever she glimpsed
an ugly broom in a café corner—
she'd shrink and disappear

Jean the Queen, Miller the Killer

To some islanders, I am an outsider—as I've only experienced Caribbean Carnival from a distance while peering through a Caribbean-American church window of stained glass. Coveting carnival's esoteric wisdom, its sacred, healing and profane effects, I have—when I have felt my most grievous and lonely—attempted to place the essence of the celebration onto small, rectangular slides in order to examine Carnival's brazen bacchanals through the lens of a tropical-mystical microscope. Still I, with great longing, could only witness the bright colors of these elusive celebrations shimmer weakly for me, tease me then disappear like foreign fireflies at twilight among the soft hymns and hallucinations emerging from a Bronx-made Jo-coconut River flowing beneath a second-hand, savory, Johnnycake moon.

I came of age in New York City, where voluptuous singers with full, sodden, sorrel-rouged lips sang inside of dark music bars, Caribbean-American dance halls and Cocoa Tea café's. I often heard my mother's childish, discordant wails—sultry, screaming for the holy spirit, then screaming for bloody murder—emerge through a certain savage Calypsonian's falsetto, his skin—beneath the floodlights hovering above the stage—the deep, rich color of an island at dusk.

My beautiful, island mother, a nurse known as Jean the Queen, Miller the Killer, sang in the choir at our Caribbean-American church. It is at this church, that she, of the gorgeous, garish Caribbean Ghetto once performed in a play about Galileo. I've witnessed Carnival's African and European enigmas whenever I spied my mother through the telescope or the looking glass as she sat alone in our row house kitchen on Sunday afternoons, playing her West African game, *Warri*—by herself—and singing Episcopalian hymns to God. In truth, I believed that Carnival—of the Caribbean-American kind—was the stairway into the heart and soul of my elegant, elusive, island mother.

(Oh Mami, Jean the Queen, Miller, the Killer, what happened deep
in the purple, bittersweet rains of The Soursop Forest?—where
a certain savage Calypsonian sang about you calling you God-
fearing, fine, formidable, yet inconsolable and offering you his
high-pitched Songbook, titled: *Falsettos for Island-Born Femme
Fatales*)

Pickney, that savage Calypsonian doesn't know me!
Mami, you said this to me,
while playing your Warri
and smoking a cigarette gently
as usual not looking at me
while I clutched my rosary—
He doesn't know you. And neither do I.
It is only when I search for my
real self in the looking-glass,
wearing your post-colonial costumes and
playing YOUR Mas'—
that I can tell, Mami
that I know you quite well

Scripture from the Siren

"Saint John!" a young woman cried out in prayer
as she hurried along Fort Road in Antigua at night.

The young woman carried a basket of universes
on her head—

"Saint John," she pleaded, *"speak to me of Shame:"*

"woeful, wooden saints and fallen figurines," he replied
as he appeared before her, then faded away,

"woeful, wooden saints and fallen figurines confessing
their sins in a scarlet, sullied streetcar—

But before we know shame, we must first know desire.

Desire is Brandy and Sherry shaken and stirred in a balmy,
southern bedroom with a wide open backdoor

a candle carried on top of a drum skin
to a naked, narrow bed

two feral figurines in a fallow farmyard
forming one exquisite fool

impious pianists in full ballrooms banging
their organs like drums

cargo ships in the sea crashing like cotton,
stimulating carnivals of coral

reading—in a parish of red light—
seductive scripture from the Siren."

"Thank you, Saint John!" the young woman
cried out in the tropical darkness—

every starry universe illuminated
in the basket she carried on her head.

One J'ouvert Morning

One J'ouvert Morning, barely a teenager, I danced all night among grown men and women, transformed into powdered, hand-painted, long-stilted, sequined, naked, horned and butterfly-winged revelers. Each reveler was full of Gods and Guinness Stout, jo-coconut milk, honey and red sorrel mixed with rum, a drink the color of wine.

We danced throughout the St. John's, Antiguan streets flanked by tiny, green, yellow and red houses and enormous shacks the color of mud and dung. There I was carousing among the light and dark-skinned trees and foul smelling sewers sweetened by the celebrations, as though I were dancing throughout my childhood spent playing with my brother and our Antiguan cousin in Bronx Park, riding our bicycles until the training wheels came off, pushing each other higher on the swings and then roller-skating along the reservoir.

Blissful and lucid after the final bacchanals of carnival, walking alone along the Secret Streets, my wings broken, skin muddy and still walking tall on my sturdy stilts, I recalled that earlier, while no one was looking out for me, I had drowned in Antigua's Half Moon Bay. I succumbed to her deceptive and soothing dark blue waters. And in my surrender to that Slumber, I kept swimming—even though I didn't know how—into the magnificent, morning light.

The Secret Streets of Saint John's

A lively baby girl, born to a dead mother inside a green, pastel shack in St. John's, Antigua, was submerged by spirits in a cask of Jo-coconut rum, then christened *Glory*—short for glorification of love and violence.

Stray dog, her horse. Her tough, bare, dark brown feet her only pair of shoes. She migrated north to a New York favela on Fordham Road and became known as Scarlet of the southern slum and a tender, tamarind-tinted tart.

Obeah-teller of unfortunate fortunes. A sultry silhouette of the sea, her teeth a flash of sugarcane coral. See her soft, sweet, currant roll belly where she works in a bakery on Flatbush Avenue, her buttered buttocks, widespread. Cuban cigars hide like refugees in her big, tight brassiere.

Famished, she devours mangos among Antigua's horniest goats, bleating, waiting to be beheaded and curried for food amid crowing, massive, ready to be cooked cocks.

American and Antiguan, *Glory* is timeless. Her headdress of candlelit ancestor altars illuminates internal passages, secret streets to her heart, lined with libraries of mystical books she longs to read in order to translate their primal poetics of pidgin and patois into wisdom for her life.

Watch her in the Villa Area—walking Fort Road to find good fortune. Watch her turn onto the Secret Streets of Saint John's, Antigua. Some streets, sacred, others, quite salacious. All are secret. Watch her carry, in a basket, an offering of fresh baked Johnnycakes to Saint John for another blessing and Revelation. *Glory*—watch her—*Hallelujah!*

Butterfly Bacchanal

A large, blue-green butterfly
hovering in the uppermost
corner of my dark bedroom

gently fluttered its delicate wings.

I sat up in bed and whistled.

The butterfly turned around—

and I saw that the butterfly was my mother.

She had returned to earth, dressed for Carnival.

My mother flew around my room and transformed
the moody space into festive, carnival grounds,

where colorful people danced about me, forgetting
every bit of pain and humiliation they had endured.

Oh, to see my mother dance—

waving her butterfly arms
moving her butterfly hips
smiling her butterfly smile

made me get out of my mourner's bed,
still a caterpillar—
and dance with her

Tiffany Osedra Miller is a Caribbean-American writer and visual artist from New York City where she teaches poetry and drawing workshops for children and senior citizens. Her work has appeared in *The New York Times, The Threepenny Review, The Jellyfish Review, Typishly* and *Palette Poetry* where she wrote and illustrated a monthly lyric essay column called, "Goatwater." which was based on her online, self-produced Caribbean Dream Carnival poetry and cartoon series of the same name. A finalist for the Calvino Prize and a finalist for the Gold Line Fiction Competition, she also wrote and illustrated the "Goatwater" chapbook, *We Need the Mask.*